BOBA JOURNAL

BOBA
JOURNAL

ARCTURUS

This edition published in 2026 by Arcturus Publishing Limited
26/27 Bickels Yard, 151–153 Bermondsey Street,
London SE1 3HA

ISBN: 978-1-3988-6807-6
AD013070NT
Supplier 29, Date 1225, PI 00012864

Printed in China

Introduction

Fill this charming journal with your hopes and dreams each morning, and then with every wonderful thing you have experienced each night. Some pages include specific prompts to help you think about what you might wish to see or what you've done that day, while others are less structured to allow you to express whatever you choose about the day ahead or the day that has been. Take a journey of whimsy with the delightful boba characters within and make every day count!

Good Morning Sunshine!

Today I am most looking forward to...

Making a Wish

Today I hope I get to...

Good Night Moon

Today was good because...

....

....

....

....

The Highlight Reel

These three things were the best bits of my day:

1. ....

2. ....

3. ....

Today I learned...

....

....

....

....

Good Morning Sunshine!

AM

Today I am going to...

Good Night Moon

PM

Today was great because...

Good Morning Sunshine!

Today I am most looking forward to...

Making a Wish

Today I hope I get to...

Good Night Moon

PM

Today was good because...

The Highlight Reel

These three things were the best bits of my day:

1.

2.

3.

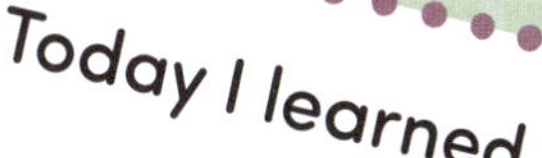

Today I learned...

AM

Good Morning Sunshine!

Today I am going to...

Good Night Moon

Today was great because...

Good Morning Sunshine!

Today I am most looking forward to...

Today I hope I get to...

PM

Good Night Moon

Today was good because...

....

....

....

....

The Highlight Reel

These three things were the best bits of my day:

1. ....

2. ....

3. ....

Today I learned...

....

....

....

....

Good Morning Sunshine!

Good Night Moon

Good Morning Sunshine!

Today I am most looking forward to...

Today I hope I get to...

Good Night Moon

Today was good because...

....

....

....

....

The Highlight Reel

These three things were the best bits of my day:

1. ....

2. ....

3. ....

Today I learned...

....

....

....

....

Good Morning Sunshine!

Today I am going to...

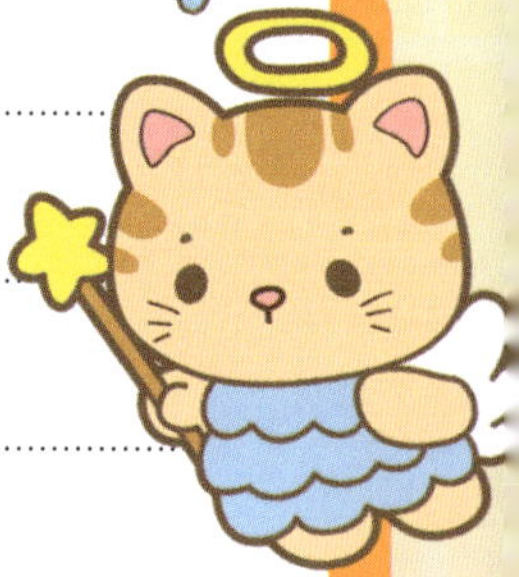

Good Night Moon

PM

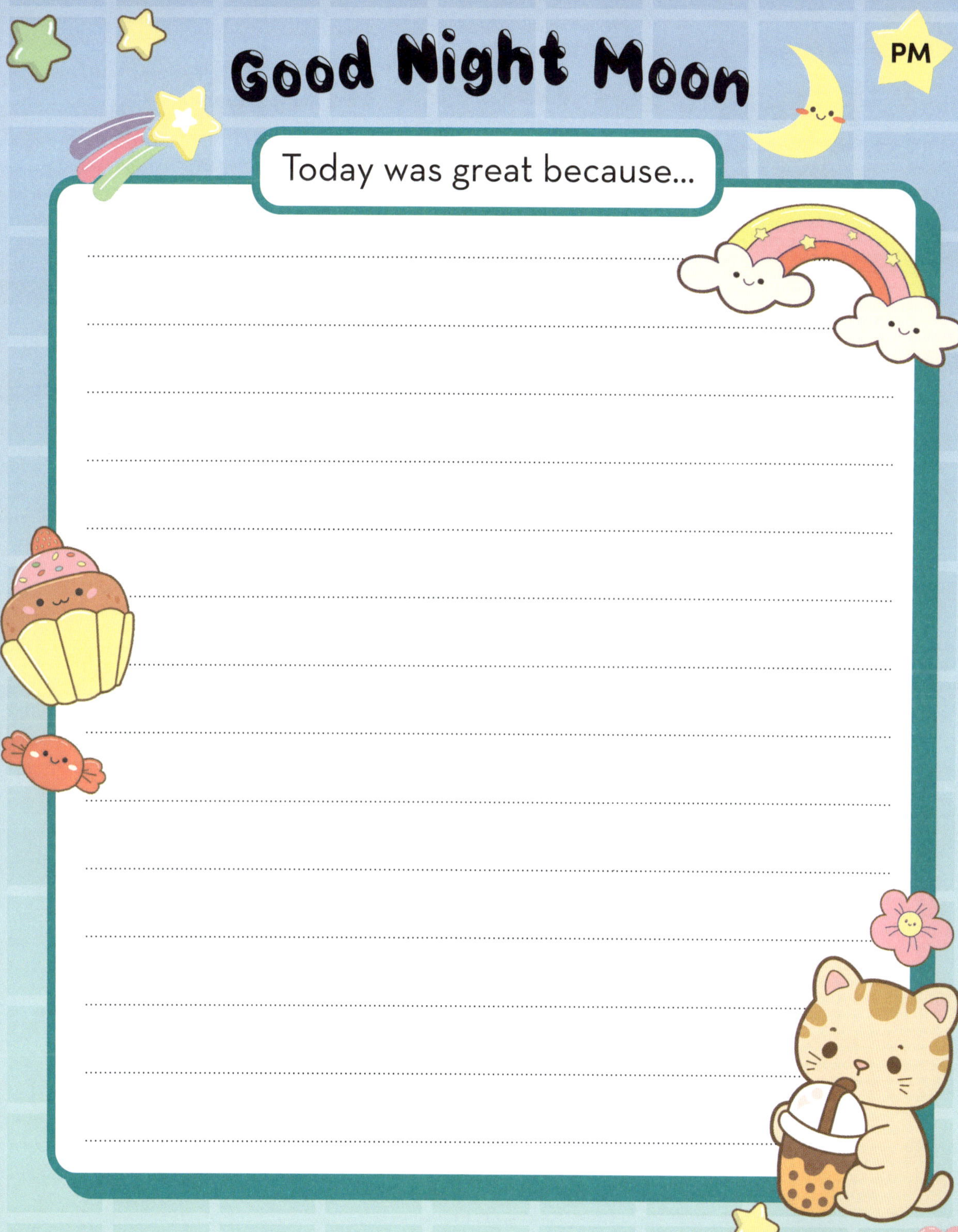

Today was great because...

Good Morning Sunshine!

Today I am most looking forward to...

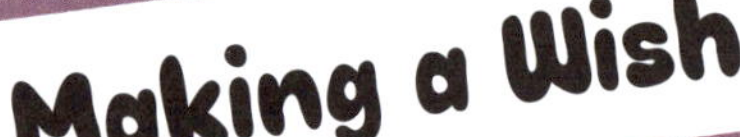

Today I hope I get to...

Good Night Moon

Today was good because...

The Highlight Reel

These three things were the best bits of my day:

1.

2.

3.

Today I learned...

Good Morning Sunshine!

Today I am going to...

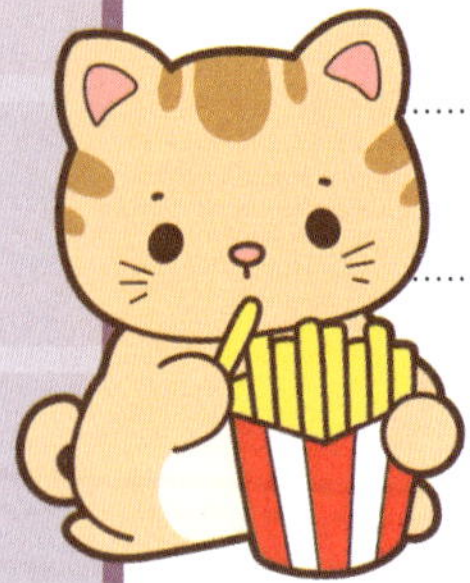

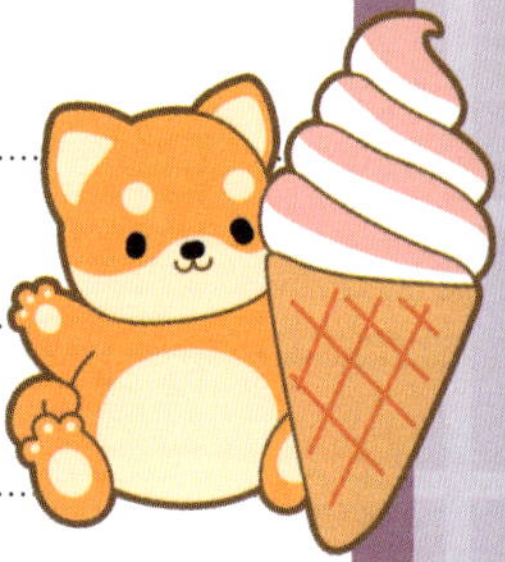

Good Night Moon

Today was great because...

Good Morning Sunshine!

Today I am most looking forward to...

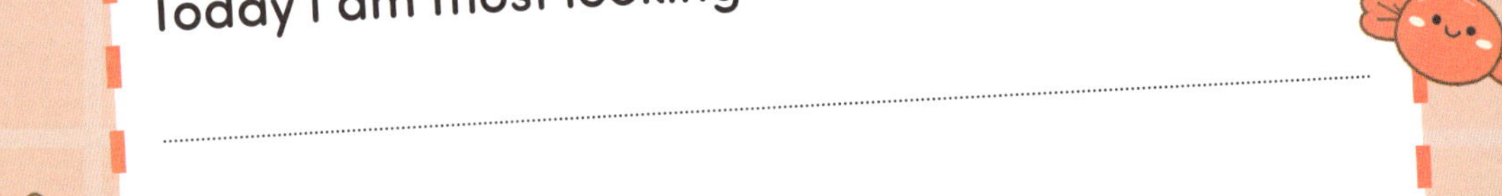

Making a Wish

Today I hope I get to...

PM

Good Night Moon

Today was good because...

....

....

....

....

The Highlight Reel

These three things were the best bits of my day:

1. ....

2. ....

3. ....

Today I learned...

....

....

....

....

Good Morning Sunshine!

Today I am going to...

Good Night Moon

PM

Today was great because...

Good Morning Sunshine!

Today I am most looking forward to...

Making a Wish

Today I hope I get to...

Good Night Moon

Today was good because...

The Highlight Reel

These three things were the best bits of my day:

1.

2.

3.

Today I learned...

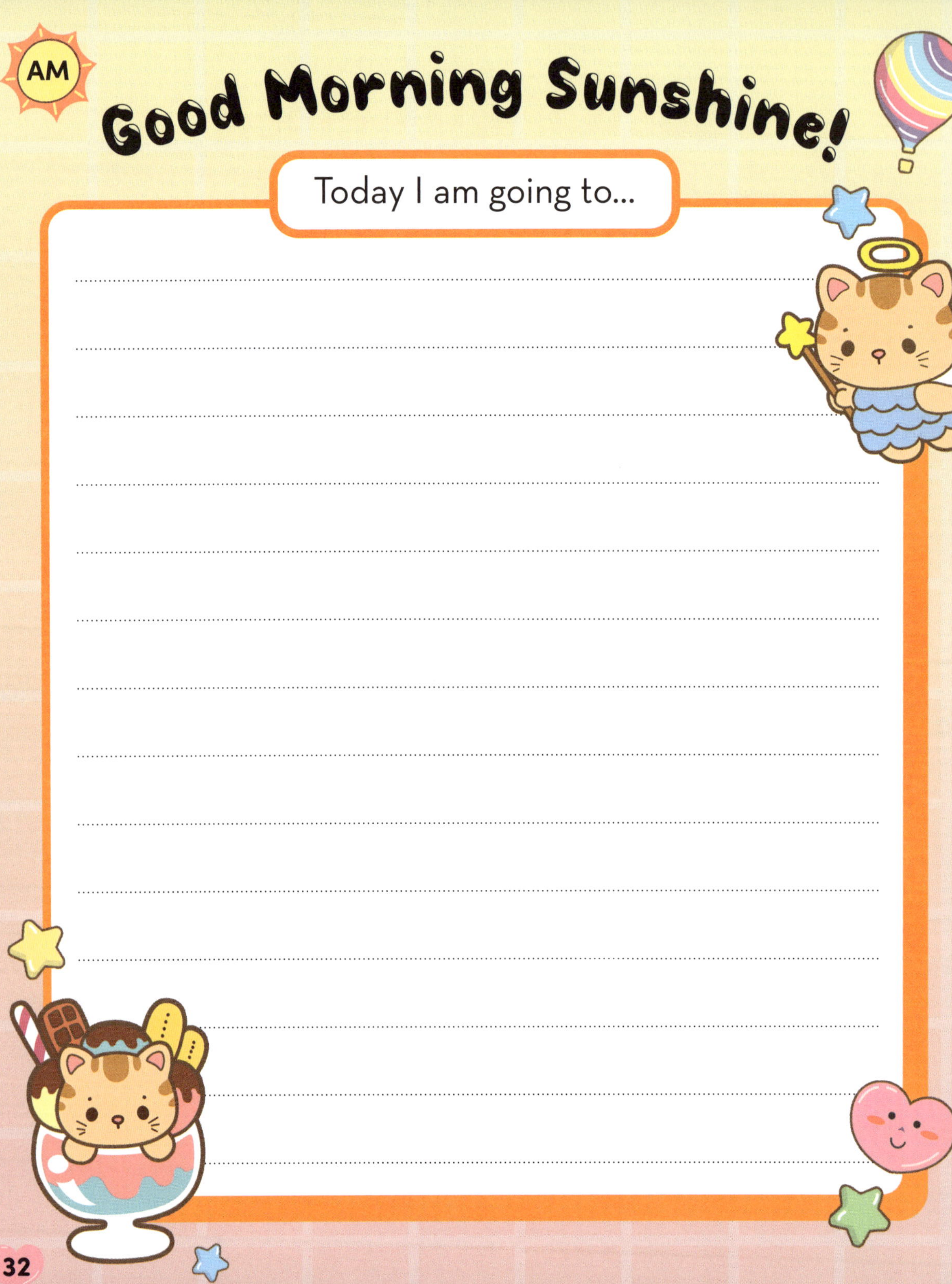

Good Morning Sunshine!

Today I am going to...

Good Night Moon

PM

Today was great because...

Good Morning Sunshine!

Today I am most looking forward to...

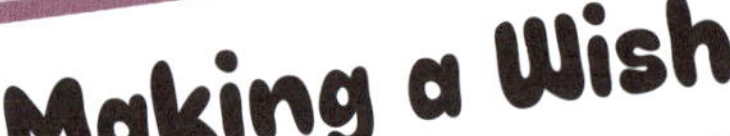

Making a Wish

Today I hope I get to...

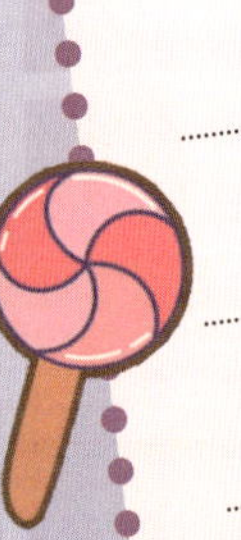

Good Night Moon

PM

Today was good because...

The Highlight Reel

These three things were the best bits of my day:

1.

2.

3.

Today I learned...

Good Morning Sunshine!

AM

Today I am going to...

Good Night Moon

Today was great because...

Good Morning Sunshine!

Today I am most looking forward to...

Making a Wish

Today I hope I get to...

Good Night Moon

Today was good because...

The Highlight Reel

These three things were the best bits of my day:

1.

2.

3.

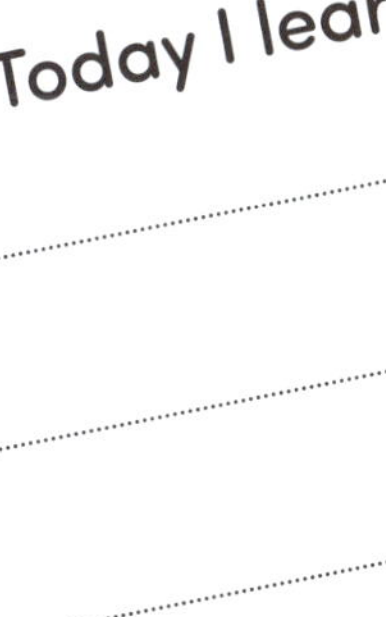

Today I learned...

Good Morning Sunshine!

Today I am going to...

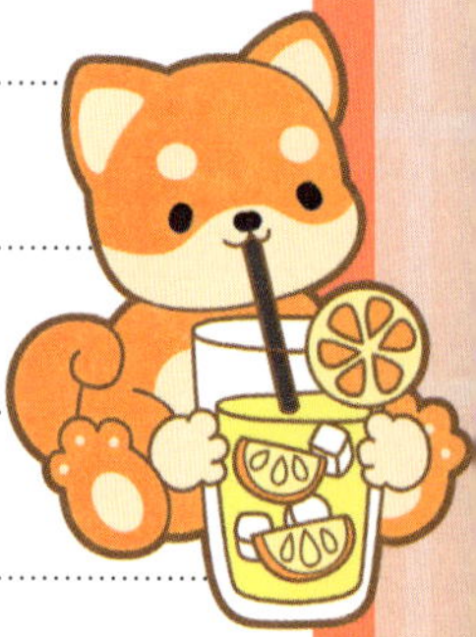

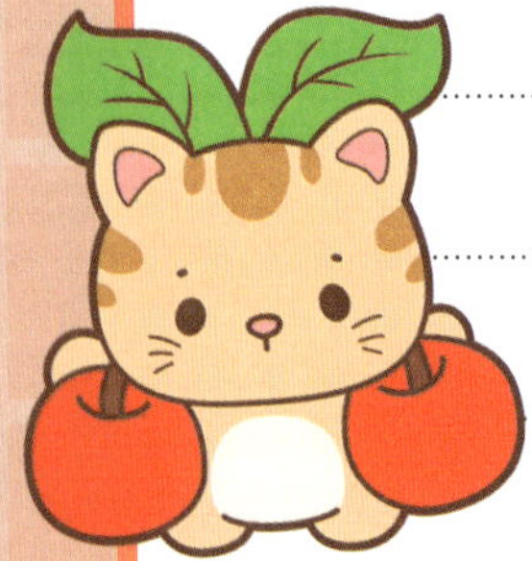

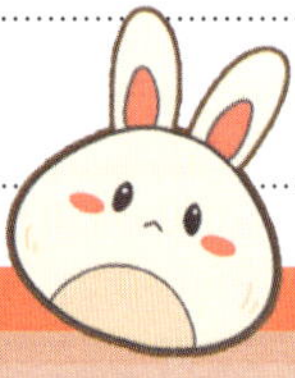

Good Night Moon

Today was great because...

Good Morning Sunshine!

Today I am most looking forward to...

Making a Wish

Today I hope I get to...

Good Night Moon

PM

Today was good because...

....

....

....

....

The Highlight Reel

These three things were the best bits of my day:

1. ....

2. ....

3. ....

Today I learned...

....

....

....

....

Good Morning Sunshine!

Today I am going to...

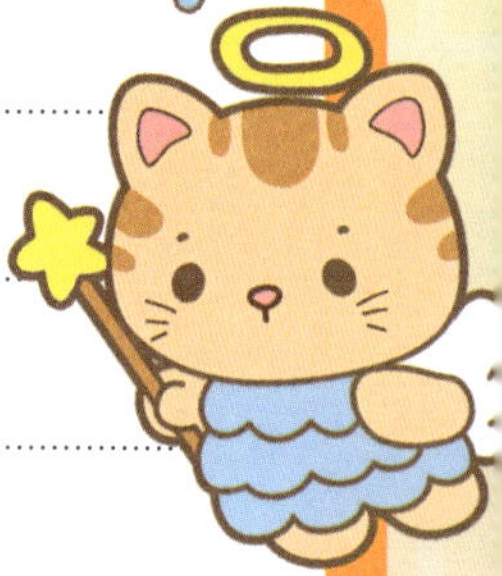

Good Night Moon

PM

Today was great because...

Good Morning Sunshine!

Today I am most looking forward to...

Making a Wish

Today I hope I get to...

Good Night Moon

PM

Today was good because...

The Highlight Reel

These three things were the best bits of my day:

1.

2.

3.

Today I learned...

AM
Good Morning Sunshine!
Today I am going to...

Good Night Moon

Today was great because...

Good Morning Sunshine!

Today I am most looking forward to...

Making a Wish

Today I hope I get to...

Good Night Moon

Today was good because...

The Highlight Reel

These three things were the best bits of my day:

1.

2.

3.

Today I learned...

Good Morning Sunshine!

Today I am going to...

Good Night Moon

Today was great because...

Good Morning Sunshine!

Today I am most looking forward to...

Making a Wish

Today I hope I get to...

Today was good because...

The Highlight Reel

These three things were the best bits of my day:

1.

2.

3.

Today I learned...

Good Morning Sunshine!

AM

Today I am going to...

PM

Good Morning Sunshine!

Today I am most looking forward to...

Today I hope I get to...

Good Night Moon

Today was good because...

....

....

....

....

The Highlight Reel

These three things were the best bits of my day:

1. ....
2. ....
3. ....

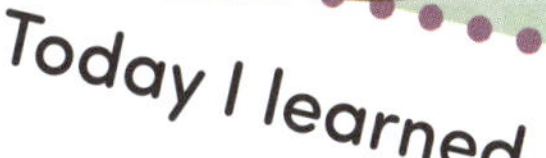

Today I learned...

....

....

....

....

....

Today I am going to...

Good Night Moon

Good Morning Sunshine!

Today I am most looking forward to...

Making a Wish

Today I hope I get to...

PM

Good Night Moon

Today was good because...

....

....

....

....

The Highlight Reel

These three things were the best bits of my day:

1. ....

2. ....

3. ....

Today I learned...

....

....

....

....

Good Morning Sunshine!

AM

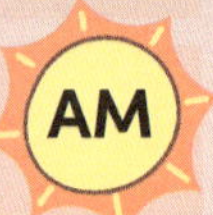

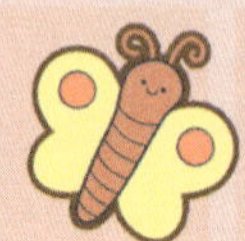

Today I am going to...

Good Night Moon

PM

Today was great because...

Good Morning Sunshine!

Today I am most looking forward to...

Making a Wish

Today I hope I get to...

PM

Good Night Moon

Today was good because...

The Highlight Reel

These three things were the best bits of my day:

1. ....

2. ....

3. ....

Today I learned...

Good Morning Sunshine!

Today I am going to...

Good Night Moon

PM

Today was great because...

AM

Good Morning Sunshine!

Today I am most looking forward to...

Making a Wish

Today I hope I get to...

Good Night Moon

PM

Today was good because...

The Highlight Reel

These three things were the best bits of my day:

1.

2.

3.

Today I learned...

Good Morning Sunshine!

Today I am going to...

Good Night Moon

Today was great because...

Good Morning Sunshine!

Today I am most looking forward to...

Making a Wish

Today I hope I get to...

Good Night Moon

PM

Today was good because...

The Highlight Reel

These three things were the best bits of my day:

1. ....

2. ....

3. ....

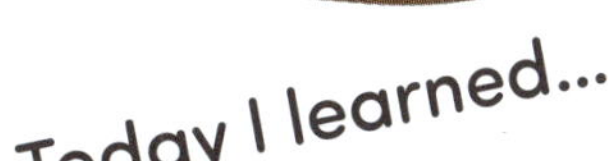

Today I learned...

Good Morning Sunshine!

Good Night Moon

Today was great because...

Good Morning Sunshine!

Today I am most looking forward to...

Making a Wish

Today I hope I get to...

Good Night Moon

Today was good because...

....

....

....

....

The Highlight Reel

These three things were the best bits of my day:

1. ....

2. ....

3. ....

Today I learned...

....

....

....

....

Good Morning Sunshine!

Today I am going to...

Good Night Moon

PM

Today was great because...

Good Morning Sunshine!

Today I am most looking forward to...

Making a Wish

Today I hope I get to...

Good Night Moon

Today was good because...

The Highlight Reel

These three things were the best bits of my day:

1.

2.

3.

Today I learned...

Today I am going to...

Good Night Moon

Today was great because...

Good Morning Sunshine!

Today I am most looking forward to...

Making a Wish

Today I hope I get to...

PM

Good Night Moon

Today was good because...

The Highlight Reel

These three things were the best bits of my day:

1.

2.

3.

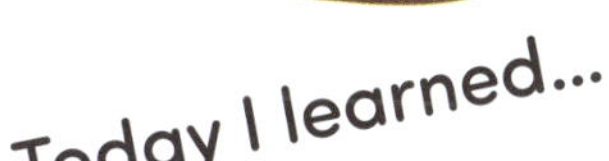

Today I learned...

Good Morning Sunshine!

Today I am going to...

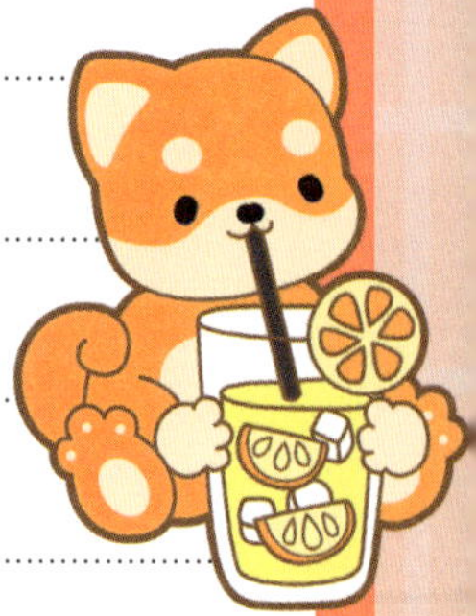

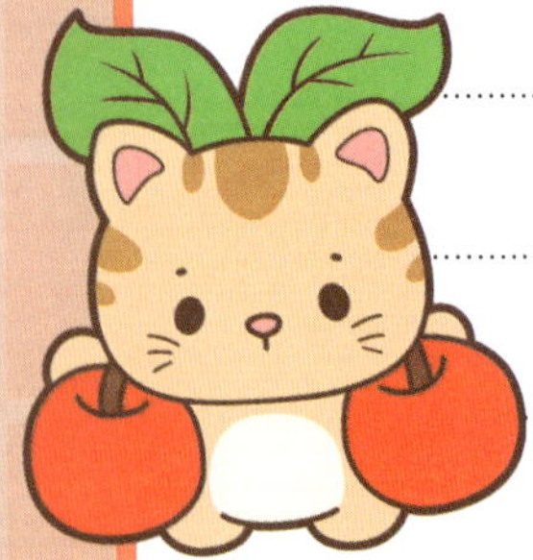

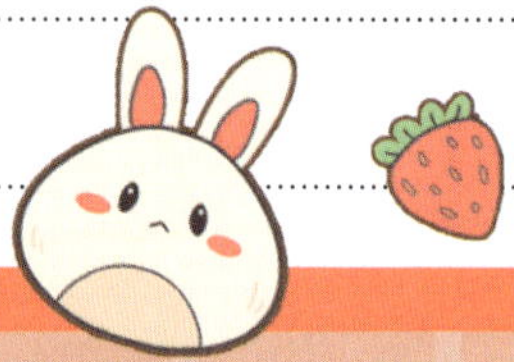

Good Night Moon

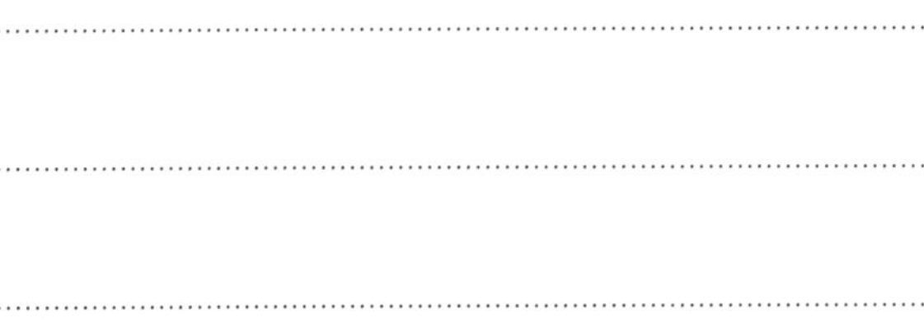

Good Morning Sunshine!

Today I am most looking forward to...

Making a Wish

Today I hope I get to...

Good Night Moon

Today was good because...

....

....

....

....

The Highlight Reel

These three things were the best bits of my day:

1. ....

2. ....

3. ....

Today I learned...

....

....

....

....

Good Morning Sunshine!

Today I am going to...

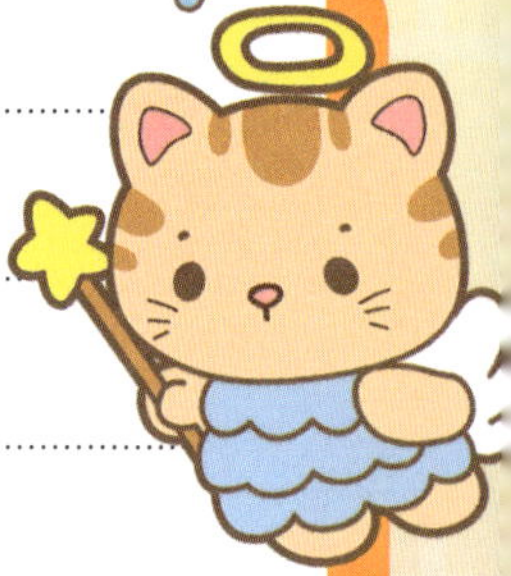

Good Night Moon

PM

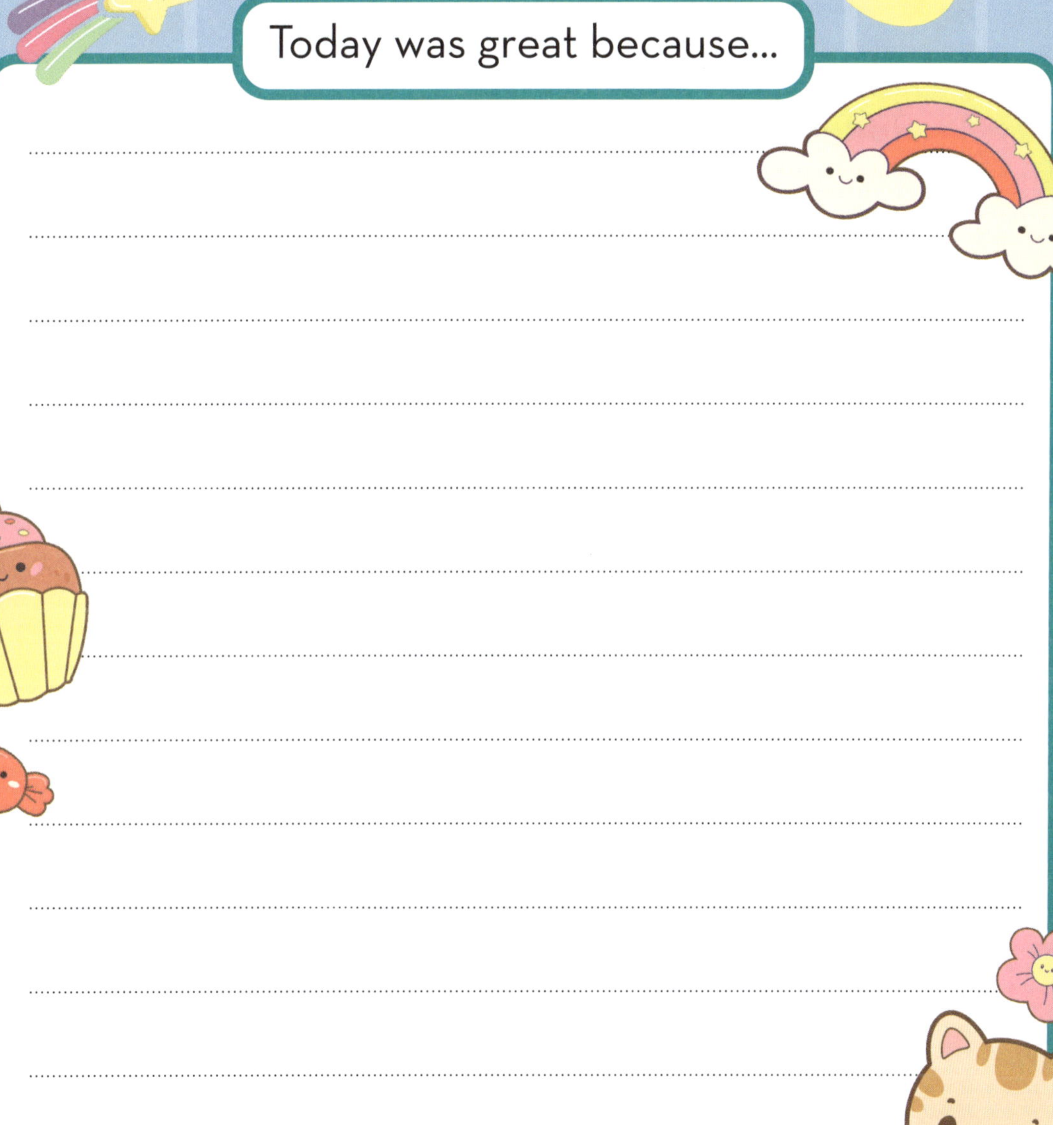

Today was great because...

Good Morning Sunshine!

Today I am most looking forward to...

Making a Wish

Today I hope I get to...

Good Night Moon

PM

Today was good because...

The Highlight Reel

These three things were the best bits of my day:

1. ....

2. ....

3. ....

Today I learned...

Good Morning Sunshine!

AM

Today I am going to...

Good Night Moon

Good Morning Sunshine!

Today I am most looking forward to...

Today I hope I get to...

Good Night Moon

Today was good because...

The Highlight Reel

These three things were the best bits of my day:

1.
2.
3.

Today I learned...

Good Morning Sunshine!

Good Night Moon

Good Morning Sunshine!

Today I am most looking forward to...

Making a Wish

Today I hope I get to...

Good Night Moon

Today was good because...

....

....

....

....

The Highlight Reel

These three things were the best bits of my day:

1. ....

2. ....

3. ....

Today I learned...

....

....

....

....

AM

Good Morning Sunshine!

Today I am going to...

Good Night Moon

PM

Today was great because...

Good Morning Sunshine!

Today I am most looking forward to...

Making a Wish

Today I hope I get to...

Good Night Moon

PM

Today was good because...

....

....

....

....

The Highlight Reel

These three things were the best bits of my day:

1. ....

2. ....

3. ....

Today I learned...

....

....

....

....

....

AM
Good Morning Sunshine!

Today I am going to...

Good Night Moon

PM

Today was great because...

Good Morning Sunshine!

Today I am most looking forward to...

Today I hope I get to...

PM

Good Night Moon

Today was good because...

The Highlight Reel

These three things were the best bits of my day:

1. ....

2. ....

3. ....

Today I learned...

Good Morning Sunshine!

Today I am going to...

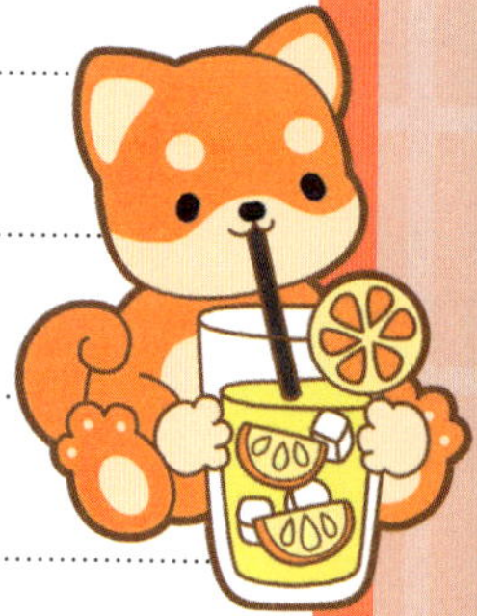

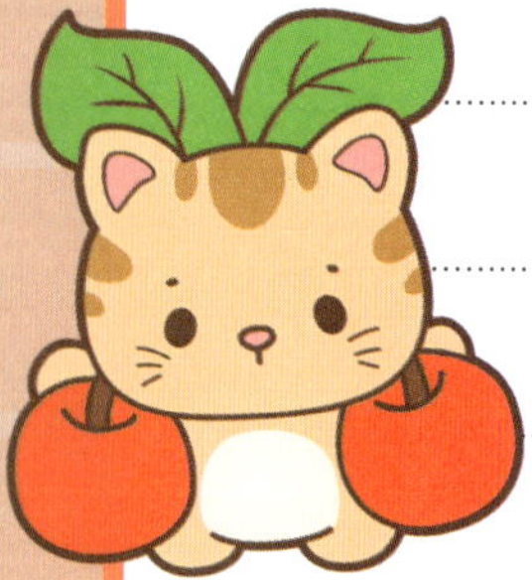

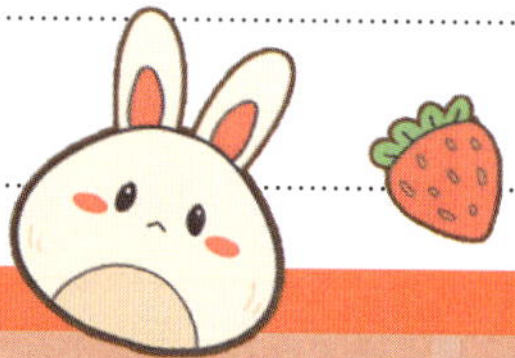

Good Night Moon

PM

Today was great because...

Good Morning Sunshine!

Today I am most looking forward to...

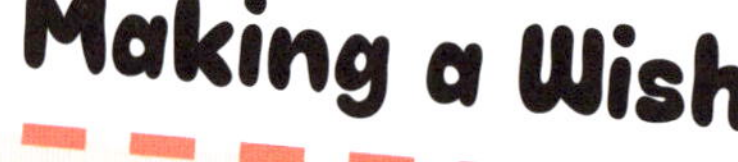

Making a Wish

Today I hope I get to...

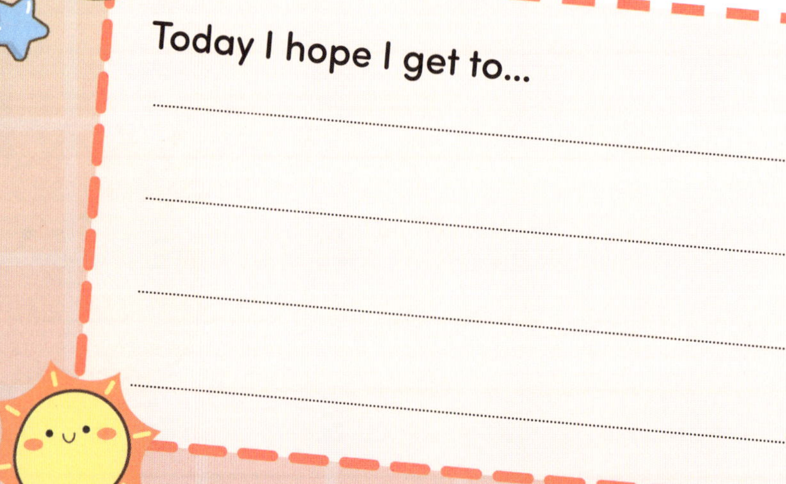

Good Night Moon

Today was good because...

The Highlight Reel

These three things were the best bits of my day:

1.

2.

3.

Today I learned...

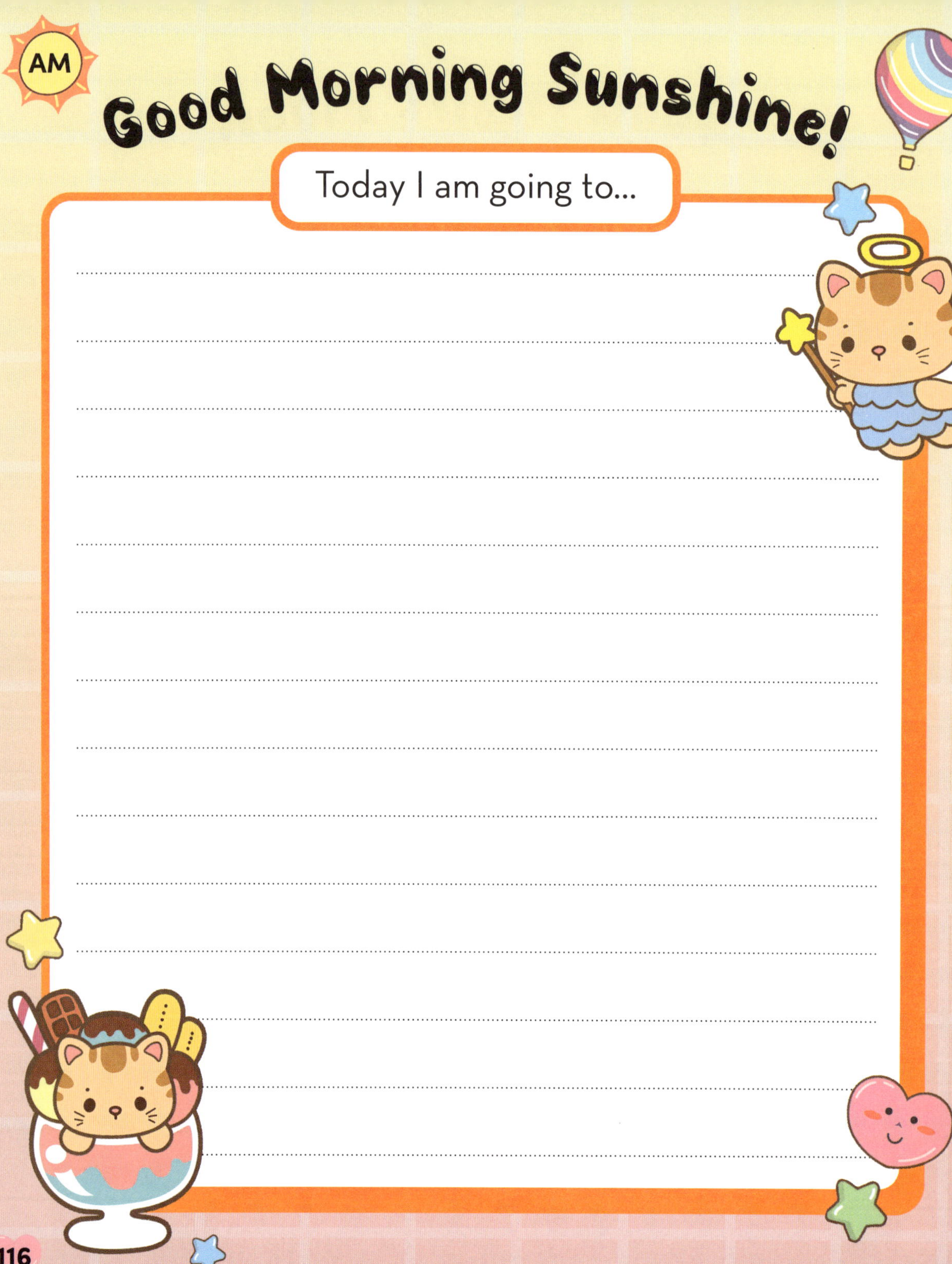

Good Morning Sunshine!

Today I am going to...

Good Night Moon

PM

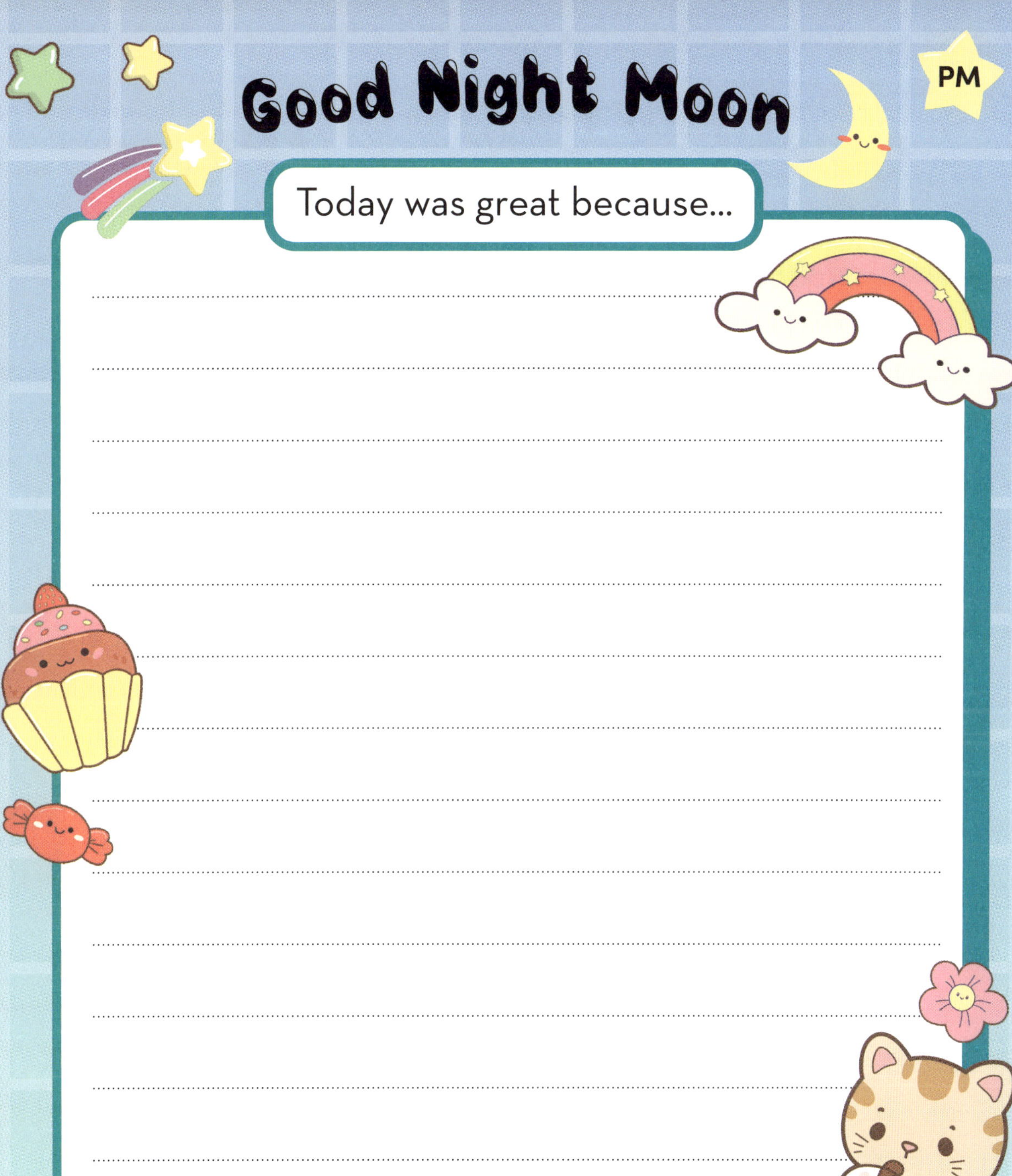

Today was great because...

Good Morning Sunshine!

Today I am most looking forward to...

Making a Wish

Today I hope I get to...

Good Night Moon

Today was good because...

The Highlight Reel

These three things were the best bits of my day:

1.

2.

3.

Today I learned...

Good Morning Sunshine!

AM

Today I am going to...

Good Night Moon

Today was great because...

Good Morning Sunshine!

Today I am most looking forward to...

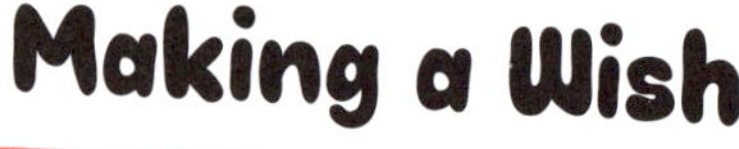

Making a Wish

Today I hope I get to...

Good Night Moon

Today was good because...

The Highlight Reel

These three things were the best bits of my day:

1.

2.

3.

Today I learned...

Good Morning Sunshine!

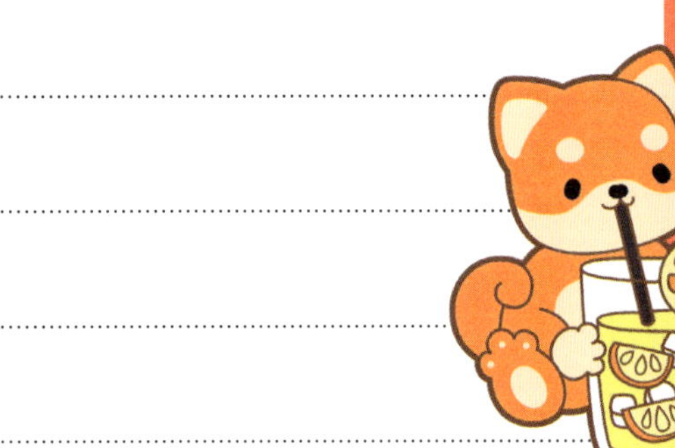

Good Night Moon

Today was great because...

Today I am most looking forward to...

Today I hope I get to...

Good Night Moon

Today was good because...

....

....

....

....

The Highlight Reel

These three things were the best bits of my day:

1. ....

2. ....

3. ....

Today I learned...

....

....

....

....